ONCE UPON A DREAM

The Imagination Chronicles

Edited By Lynsey Evans

First published in Great Britain in 2024 by:

Young Writers
Remus House
Coltsfoot Drive
Peterborough
PE2 9BF
Telephone: 01733 890066
Website: www.youngwriters.co.uk

FOREWORD

Welcome Reader, to a world of dreams.

For Young Writers' latest competition, we asked our writers to dig deep into their imagination and create a poem that paints a picture of what they dream of, whether it's a make-believe world full of wonder or their aspirations for the future.

The result is this collection of fantastic poetic verse that covers a whole host of different topics. Let your mind fly away with the fairies to explore the sweet joy of candy lands, join in with a game of fantasy football, or you may even catch a glimpse of a unicorn or another mythical creature. Beware though, because even dreamland has dark corners, so you may turn a page and walk into a nightmare!

Whereas the majority of our writers chose to stick to a free verse style, others gave themselves the challenge of other techniques such as acrostics and rhyming couplets. We also gave the writers the option to compose their ideas in a story, so watch out for those narrative pieces too!

Each piece in this collection shows the writers' dedication and imagination – we truly believe that seeing their work in print gives them a well-deserved boost of pride, and inspires them to keep writing, so we hope to see more of their work in the future!

CONTENTS

Memphis 60
Norah Maloney (9) 61
Jacob Whitrick (9) 62
Connie Preston (8) 63
Alyssa Rose Godfrey (9) 64
Skye Oakley (9) 65

Midfield Primary School, St Paul's Cray

Jarrin Hussain (10) 66
Esther Ayomikun Iranloye (10) 68
Charlotte Muller (9) 69
Emily Spittles (10) 70
Sophie Anderson (9) 71
Hollie Anna Rynne (10) 72
Tony Friend (10) 73
Zak Souami (10) 74
Anishwar Chellappan (10) 75
Florence Wright (10) 76

Mobberley CE Primary School, Mobberley

Liberty Taylor (9) 77
Emily McIntyre (8) 78
Emily Sellars-Rooney (10) 80
Louisa Todor (8) 81
Hope Jones (8) 82
Hettie Taylor (10) 83
Frankie Cummings (8) 84
Zach Saunders (11) 85
Ed Hargreaves (11) 86
Matilda Hargreaves (9) 87
Nat Kirkwood (11) 88
Charlotte Northover (7) 89
Dylan Waterfield (11) 90
Ellen Jones (11) 91
Daisy Middleditch (8) 92
Archie Murrell (8) 93
Henry Taylor (11) 94
Amelia-Rose Stapleton (11) 95
Olivia Marshall (8) 96
Poppy Nicholson (8) 97

Liviana Baines (8) 98
Poppy Norbury (10) 99
Ronny Owens (8) 100
Juliette Hurley (10) 101

North Town Primary School, Taunton

Coral-Olivia Brown (9) 102
Jasmine Mcevansoneya (8) 103
Jack Rose (8) 104
Carys Perry (9) 105
Rufus Ennals (8) 106
Alexandra Slonska De Ostoja (10) 107
Areeya Ketnil (8) 108
Sonia Nikisina (8) 109
Harrison Dorrill (8) 110
Luna Raby (8) 111
Alina Meshack (8) 112
Jewel Jithu (9) 113
Joey Sawyer (9) 114
Kayla Nyika (8) 115
Daria Marita (7) 116
Maja Wawrzyniak (8) 117
Abhinav Binu (8) 118
Okitha Ranaweera (7) 119
Hugo 120

Stanton Harcourt CE Primary School, Stanton Harcourt

Molly Bungay (9) 121
Tenuki Lokugamhewa (8) 122
Georgie Day (9) 123
Olga Jastrzebska (7) 124
Livi Brown (9) 125
Elissa Hammonds (8) 126

The King's School, Gloucester

Isabella Frederick-Martinez (10) 127
Abbi Navaratnam (10) 128
Sabrina Stratford (10) 131
Eliza Humber (10) 132

Harvey Dodson (10)	134
Oliver Odufuwa (9)	136
Molly Smart (10)	137
Fred Beavon-Keenan (10)	138
Sebastian Le Page (9)	140
Theodore Currie (10)	142
Kitty Dare (9)	143
Evangeline Walker (9)	144
James Hargreaves (9)	146
Tom Holliday (10)	147
Josiah Manboard (9)	148
Liesl Bier (10)	149
Rosie Worthington (10)	150
Charlie Elsby Harfield (10)	151
Caspar Smith (9)	152
Luca Grosch (9)	154
Amelia van Wyk (9)	155
Freddie Haighway (10)	156
Zac Yousif Spilsbury (10)	157
Alfie Spokes (10)	158
Eddie Skivington (10)	159
Imogen Halliday	160
Rhys Walker (10)	161

THE CREATIVE WRITING

Wish Wonderland

W here in the world do dreams come true?
I n a place that is magical as can be,
S ome people say it's magical or dreamy,
H iding in a forest waiting to be found,

W ish wonderland,
O n top of the sugar waterfalls are giant marshmallows,
N ine Irish dancers chasing beautiful swallows,
D ancing from night until dawn,
E veryone is welcome to see them perform,
R ainbows light up the sky and bring us joy,
L et's go hand in hand and explore this wonderland,
A nd when the night starts to fall, popping candy stars fill the sky,
N obody needs to feel alone,
D arkness glistens against the luminous.

Valentina Bonsignore (9)
Abington Vale Primary School, Cliftonville

The Enchanted Forest

Step into the forest, a whole world awaits you,
Under the cotton candy trees that are flowing with
fluffy cotton candy, as pink as cherry blossom.
A carpet of bluebells lies upon the perfect green grass.
Listen to the sounds of the birds and feel the frosty
earth crunching under your feet.
The forest is full of rustling and whispering as it slowly
comes to life.
Spring is here!
Some branches are covered in blossom, splashes of
pink and white.
Most of the forest floor has become a huge mattress of
bluebells, more beautiful than any painting.
Bears take a swim in the cool, soothing blue stream
surrounded by sugar plums,
As birds of all kinds fly in the joyful, springtime breeze.

Tripti Peter (9)
Abington Vale Primary School, Cliftonville

Achieving My Dreams

My dance has been famous for years,
I wanted to do another one again!
Twirl, flick hair, jump!
I posted it and over one hundred people hated it,
They said, "Boo, ugly dance!" and I missed being popular.
I deleted the dance I did and then did it
Again and again and again, and I finally made it!
It got over one hundred likes and positive comments.
I was so happy, I could follow my dreams.
Let me tell you something,
At first try, success doesn't always work.
Remember this,
Follow your dream everywhere it goes,
If you're feeling down, try again.
Never give up!

Princess Idahosa (9)
Abington Vale Primary School, Cliftonville

My Dream

I could see my wings flapping like magical waves.
A round black clock around me,
Which made my hand warm.
The magical brown wand, made me strong.

A lovely dragon,
Coloured like a bright sun,
Slept next to me.

Then I saw a big school,
But it looked like a mansion.

A beautiful fairy came to me,
And said, "Hi, I am Amly.
What's your name?"
"Hi, my name is Nessa."
I was so excited,
Before I could say anything,
She disappeared.
When I woke up,
It was all a dream.
But at least, I had a nice dream.

Nessa Jose (9)
Abington Vale Primary School, Cliftonville

Stars

Is it the way they glisten,
That makes it feel like they listen?

In the bright night sky, the stars shining oh so bright,
Thinking about how many lives they've watched.

The stars make us feel all glowy inside,
When the sun takes over, the stars snooze,
But when they awake, they sway to and fro,
Small stars, and even big ones too!
Stars are so excellent in everything they do,
Dancing and prancing and even snoozing too.

I wonder where the stars go, when it reaches the break of dawn,
Then, when the time reaches, the sun takes over.

Rukky Ilobi (9)
Abington Vale Primary School, Cliftonville

The Boy's Kite

It was a windy night,
The stars were very bright,
A boy was playing with his kite.
The kite was going high,
Above the midnight sky,
The boy didn't know the kite could fly high,
High, almost reaching the stars in the sky.
It reached the sky,
The boy was surprised that it went really high.
He went home and had a nice time!

Mihran Munim (8)
Abington Vale Primary School, Cliftonville

Monsters

M onsters are very spooky, scary,

O val shaped,

N ew monsters appear every day,

S limy, spooky, scary, fat,

T errifying creatures every night,

E normous gigantic like to fight,

R ed, blue, yellow, bright,

S lightly less friendly at night.

Arthur Avramenko (8)
Abington Vale Primary School, Cliftonville

Dancing Devils

D ancing around in a circus on the stage when I'm in a rage,

A round on the beach in the middle of a dream,

N ice things for me in the dark and in the park,

C oming at me are cackling clowns bouncing around the rounds,

I can see it is dark, but dogs like to bark,

N ow I'm happy, I will show you if you want to know it,

G etting my make-up on so I'm ready, and I'll get a teddy.

D evils dancing under the light at night,

E very dance good, but my heart can't keep up but the sheep help me up,

V ery many people are coming and I feel like running,

I s this meant to be good, because I'm stood with a fake smile,

L et me say goodbye as I sigh.

Nola Knox (9)

Hadrian Park Primary School, Wallsend

One Bad Night

One mysterious night,
There was a blurry light,
It shone bright and clear,
But nobody could hear
My frightening screams,
"Help, help it's me!"
A big black hole,
Nobody to call,
Am I dead?
Is that also someone under my bed?
I might be dead,
Should I just flee, like a bee?
My knees begin to shake,
My bed is like an earthquake.
Of course, it's a black hole,
But not like I've seen before.
I begin to stress,
How did I get into this mess?
Yes, it's beginning to fade away,
Hooray! Hooray! Hooray!
Goodbye for now, let's hope next time I don't see a
killer clown.

Harry Alcock (10)
Hadrian Park Primary School, Wallsend

Imagination

O pen a world of imagination,
N o cloud in sight,
C ats fly like a kite,
E lephants light as a feather,

U nder the sea is where you will find
P ufferfish explode with fireworks,
O nly you have the power of imagination,
N o rain in the forecast,

A magical life is all you need,

D on't doubt dreams,
R eindeer fly so high and high,
E very star has a perfect smile,
A ll my dreams are in my head, like a monster under my bed,
M um walks in and suddenly it's gone. Was it a dream?

Luca Wells (10)
Hadrian Park Primary School, Wallsend

The Lost Island

I'm falling, deep deep down,
It's filled with darkness and gloom,
I look around, I'm in shock, I'm not in my room,
I crash down on the ground, nothing in sight,
I open my eyes, it looks quite nice,
It feels strange, it feels weird, does my head have lice?
Palm trees on one side, mountains on another,
Ruins with stairs, a condor on the cliff,
He swoops down, down to the ground,
He zigzags, comes down, and picks me up,
Beak on shirt, talons on shoes,
I think this is the end,
I jump up, look around, and realise it was just in my
head!

Toby Williams (10)
Hadrian Park Primary School, Wallsend

Nightmare

N othing happens until I get into a dream,
I see a black figure in the sky,
G lancing left and right, all I see are black clouds,
H ow could this happen? Hope this is a dream.
T hud! Lightning hits around me,
M y heart pounds in my chest,
A fter a bit it gets worse, the thunder,
R unning as fast as I can to get away,
E vil eyes stare at me, goosebumps envelop my body,
S uddenly I wake up, to see I'm nice and safe.

Adem Karakoyun (10)
Hadrian Park Primary School, Wallsend

Monsters

M y mouth dropped, my ears popped. My body's rumbling.

O n my bed, I'm very scared. All I hear is mumbling.

N o one there with a pair. No one there to scare.

S top, stop, stop, I shouted in despair.

T here I was in my bed. All I could see were flashes of red.

E verything in my head, all I wanted to was fled.

R ealised I think it might be my sister, playing the drums.

S trolling out of my bed, I said you're beating on the bed.

Jude Blacklock (10)
Hadrian Park Primary School, Wallsend

Dancer

D ancing is nice,
A nd so are mice,
N early every dancer fights,
C an you not worry, I'm alright,
E verywhere is like a dream,
R eady to go on the beam.

P ractising all night,
R apidly turning light,
A beautiful dress,
N o need to stress,
C urrently making a twirl,
E rrrm! This music makes me whirl,
R epeatedly making me dance.

Chloe Smith (10)
Hadrian Park Primary School, Wallsend

Dessert Dragons

Every night I lie in bed,
Hundreds of thoughts running through my head.
The atmosphere glows as bright as the sun,
While dragons dance around having fun.
As they dazzle like a star so bright,
They see the delicious desserts in sight.
Is that a cupcake? Looks yummy!
Spinning and twirling desserts in their tummy,
The moon flashes with a glowing beam,
Suddenly I wake - it was just a dream!

Amber Brown
Hadrian Park Primary School, Wallsend

Conservation

I was with my mam and we were in a tall building
And I could feel it had a huge ceiling
It turns out it was a conservation and my teacher was
here and proud
And a moving elephant that was pretty loud.
Trumpet! Trumpet! Trumpet!
Then I saw the sea turtles, but my mind went damp
As I thought they were cramped
But like a portal, there was a world of green and turtles
And I was so happy
The sky was now night purple.

Oliver Riley (10)
Hadrian Park Primary School, Wallsend

Space Dog

S ome of them aren't normal, that might surprise you
P ut treats out for their wisdom upon you
A t last leave a Milky Bar out, yummy
C ome at night to see the dog
E very single dog had lots of powers

D on't give them fairy pets or chomp
O r you will get punished by ghosts
G ood luck with the space dogs.

Jax Asiamah (10)
Hadrian Park Primary School, Wallsend

Dinosaurs

D inosaur's land is a cool place
I suddenly get there
N ever been this far from home before
O h! I'm here, I am scared
S o I meet a T-rex who helps me
A nd I met a pterodactyl that helps me too
U namazing when you're lost
R oarsome or unroarsome when you have to leave
S uddenly I am in bed.

Iona Hields (10)
Hadrian Park Primary School, Wallsend

Animals

A s I lay in bed stars so bright
N ot knowing what would happen that night
I watch as they tumble about
M onkey letting out a joyful shout
A hippo, a cat, is that a giraffe having a laugh?
L emur, lion, having a bath
S and burying my feet, dolphin waving from a mile
away hoping I can come another day!

Phoebe Evans (9)
Hadrian Park Primary School, Wallsend

Surf's Up

S ound asleep in my comfy bed,

U p and ready to have fun.

R eady, set, go and I am off.

F linging the surfboard into the waves.

I n the barrel, I can't escape.

N obody can see me flexing my skills,

G unning to my parents, to tell them what I've done, they don't trust me, what a bum.

Joshua Fryer Lomana (9)

Hadrian Park Primary School, Wallsend

Football

F orever a favourite game of mine,

O kay, we're losing but that is fine,

O h no, they scored again,

T eamwork needed, I'm going insane,

B ellowing screams from the crowd,

A s soon as we score, I am so proud,

L oud screams from the fans

L oads desperately waving their hands.

Scarlett Pearce (10)

Hadrian Park Primary School, Wallsend

Space Fairies

Shooting stars in the air,
Space fairies everywhere!
Surrounding me from left to right,
They won't leave me in the night.
Bouncing around on the moon,
Listening to a funky tune.
The sun is now ready to rise,
It must be time to say goodbye!
Goodbye fairies, I must rush,
Although I can say, this was lush!

Bethany Dunn (10)
Hadrian Park Primary School, Wallsend

Football

F ans cheering wildly,

O ff we go onto the pitch,

O ptimistic managers looking at me,

T oon Toon Black and White Army,

B ack on the ball, we score,

A nd the score is 1-0,

L et's go and score again,

L earn from the GOATs (Messi and Ronaldo Snr).

Jack Myers (10)
Hadrian Park Primary School, Wallsend

A Stadium As Big As Ten Whales

The boiling wind stroked my skin,
As I kicked the ball,
The sweat dripped like an F1 car
Soon *pop!*
Out of the blue, thick ghost snakes appeared,
A person stepped out of the smoke,
Michael Jackson!
I jumped out of my bed,
I thought it was my time to go!

Jamie Bartten (10)
Hadrian Park Primary School, Wallsend

Pirate

P irates fighting left and right,

I jump back and take a mighty swing,

R hh me mates, we have won da battle,

A bottle of rum for de win,

T he fifth bottle of rum for de win, now it's five,

E ee now it's time for us to go.

Mason Simons (10)
Hadrian Park Primary School, Wallsend

Alien

Once I woke up in my bed
And I saw a big alien head
Five enormous googly eyes
Had this landed from the sky?
Jumping in my bath
Having a laugh
Blowing all around
How has this got to the ground?
Now I have to say goodbye
There it goes in the sky.

Blake Hatton (9)
Hadrian Park Primary School, Wallsend

The Mini Monkey

Can you believe what I saw today,
A little monkey, hanging from the tree,
As her friend began climbing,
Her other friends were just watching,
One was reading,
One was sleeping and one was filming.
But then, she realised it was all a dream.

Elizabeth Buckton (10)
Hadrian Park Primary School, Wallsend

Football History

F ootball players,
O me lads,
O ut the Premier League they go,
T oon Toon,
B lack and White Army,
A nd all lads and lasses,
L oud crowd,
L aughter, crowd all around.

Luke Erskine (9)
Hadrian Park Primary School, Wallsend

Frisbee Far Away

Once upon a sunny day
A Frisbee lay upon the bay
I picked it up, throwing it out of sight
I gazed upon the sky, it was a surprising glimpse
What I could see, you could not believe
Saturn had two rings, now it has one.

Harry Cowely (10)
Hadrian Park Primary School, Wallsend

Once Upon A Nightmare

N ightmares aren't good but one quickly became a blight

E ver since I was no younger than two, this has given me a fright.

V ery into the night lying in bed with my parents,

E uphoria of scares made me want to run errands.

R ight with that thought, the frights were about to start,

G one was the usual and came a monster who was smart,

O ut there, I saw him with a bloodstained saw,

N ow I was next, I definitely didn't want more.

N ext came the realisation of the leg-chopping beast

A fter all that, my legs could make a yummy feast.

G reat! I thought, whilst my legs were being chopped,

I t was not real and all of the pain was stopped.

V indication was what I wanted from this horrible man,

E ither it was the horror or the moving van.

Y es, I'm correct, he wanted to move here,

O ther than that, it gave me fear.

U p I went, after that horror,

U p I woke up in the middle of nowhere called Cowour.

P ersonally, it was a moor and I even saw the core!

Jack Raftery (11)

Higher Failsworth Primary School, Failsworth

Superpowers

I've always dreamed about superpowers,
Oh how fun,
To hold the sun,
Or fly above the flowers.
If I had a pick, I'd choose electricity,
And use it above the vicinity.
But when there's trouble down below,
I'd have to say, "No! No!"
And help all those who need,
While also helping those who plead.
When sun arises, they'll see the star,
Who is me, only I'm seen from afar.
From Russia all the way to the UK,
I'm a hero, do I even have to say?
And when there's a villain or even more,
I add them into my defeated score,
While still defending the streets,
From any villains, mostly weak.
So keep this in your head or dream,
And tell anyone who seeks me: the seen,
That is me, The Super Bean.

Bailey Griffin (10)
Higher Failsworth Primary School, Failsworth

In My Dreams

Once upon a dream, I flew across the midnight sky with fluffy unicorns
Once upon a dream, I was a scary bat, hanging upside down
Once upon a dream, I fluttered as a fairy in an enchanted forest
Once upon a dream, I was a cat, chasing a mouse who had stolen my toy!
Once upon a dream, I ran through hills rounding sheep as a sheepdog
Once upon a dream, I was a famous footballer, scoring goals for fun
Once upon a dream, I was a teacher teaching my students
Once upon a dream, I was a businessman with important work
Once upon a dream, I was an astronaut floating in outer space
Once upon a dream, I was a nurse helping the injured and sick
Once upon a dream, I was a rich man getting showered with money
Once upon a dream, I was a dancer dancing in front of millions.

Farryll Wren (11)
Higher Failsworth Primary School, Failsworth

Paradise

As I drift off to sleep, I dream into paradise
As I hear the sea whirling inside my ear
I open my eyes to see a mocktail standing by my sleeve
I lie right back into the breeze and spot the waves clear
and clean
I stand up and to my pure amazement, a waiter comes
over and says,
"Good evening, I hope you will enjoy your stay at the
Grand Hotel in Marbay."
I am in shock as I walk inside the greatest, most
breathtaking hotel room in my life
It has a sauna and a super-king bed too!
I have to go to the pool and sunbathe all day in the
cool
I am about to go to a buffet but on the horizon, I hear
"Millie, Millie! Wake up for school!"
I look at my mum in despair and say,
"Awh Mum, five more minutes."

Millie Jackson (11)
Higher Failsworth Primary School, Failsworth

The Race

I was heading to bed when a thought crept into my head
Will the ribbon on the medal be red?
Will I win the dreaded race or will I go at a slow pace?
I should probably get some rest
So that tomorrow I look my best.

Suddenly, I appeared at the leisure centre
Wearing a swimming costume with a hole in the centre
I was feeling nervous and scared
I looked at the other races whilst they glared

Suddenly, I heard, "Poppy, wake up! The race is today!
Remember, it's the 3rd of May"
So was this just a dream
Or will I have a race again?

Poppy Shaw (10)
Higher Failsworth Primary School, Failsworth

A Weird Dream

As I sleep tight
My eyes don't put up a fight
I stoop into a dream
Out of this world, it seems
A completely barren land
That could use a bit of sand?
"Why does it look like a hand?"
In the far distance, I can see
A giraffe as tall as me
Yet the land was as cold as Antarctica in a fridge
But wait, the land wasn't barren
A house made of spiders
However, it looked solid.
As I tried to enter
A voice shouted,
"Wake up for school, *now!*"
It was my dad.

Elliot Ogbeide (11)
Higher Failsworth Primary School, Failsworth

Dreams And Frights

I am a knight, filled with fright,
I am a hero, I came from zero,
I am a fighter, you shall find no mind brighter,
I am a fairy, but I feel quite wary,
All my dreams and all my frights,
Keep me up through the nights,
They make me happy,
Scared and sad,
Not all dreams are good,
They can sometimes be bad,
But just remember,
Before you wake Mum and Dad,
You shall wake again,
Back in bed,
Then it's back off to the land of dreams,
But just watch out for Mr Screams!

Megann Watson (10)
Higher Failsworth Primary School, Failsworth

Friends

I had a dream about my friends
We laughed and played all day long
We played skipping and hopscotch
Oh and hula hooping too.
We never argued but when we did,
We always forgave each other.
I love my friends and they love me.
On weekends, we text, call or hang out.
I have known them for a very long time now.
I hope we are friends forever and never get separated.
My friends are amazing, kind and smart too.
I have many dreams about my friends.
And I know you do too.

Willow Raggett (10)
Higher Failsworth Primary School, Failsworth

Haunted Dream

As I walk through the haunted house
I hear a freaky shout.
Walking towards the bed
It smelled like something was dead.
I needed to get out of here.
I didn't know what else would appear.
I ran as fast as I could.
I tripped over a piece of wood.
Then something appeared
A monster with a big ear.
Then my mum shouted, "Wakey, wakey!"
I was so happy that was a dream.

Logan Ninian (10)
Higher Failsworth Primary School, Failsworth

Anxious Cup Desire

As I slept, trying to get up
Hoping to win this great cup
This is my big, final game
To show them what I've became
I need goals more, more and more
Possibly I could just score
This is the end of the line
May 4th, the big deadline
This trophy will be claimed
It'll be our biggest aim
All eyes are on this massive match
Running down the field patch.

Ethan Berete (11)
Higher Failsworth Primary School, Failsworth

Dreams Are Just Dreams

Dreams can be good,
dreams can be bad,
but the best ones won't be sad.
It will be great,
there will be no hate.
I could have powers,
I won't need any showers.
I would be a pirate,
and change the climate.
I could be a superstar,
and drive supercars.
But in the end,
I wake up
and remember
dreams are just dreams.

Rory Fairley (10)
Higher Failsworth Primary School, Failsworth

Flying Pig

"There's a pig in the sky,"
shouted the boy
"It might be a toy,"
yelled the flying cow
"Calm down, the flying pig is just like us."
In the bright blue sky, the pig flies
"Look in the clouds."
Many more flying pigs lay
As the other pigs glided
Through the bright blue sky.

Janae Nolan (10)
Higher Failsworth Primary School, Failsworth

Space Clowns

If you need space get some pace
If you're scared of clowns don't be down
If you have some time make it rhyme
If it's April be faithful
If it's home time it's go time
If you're grey get some day!
If now it's horrid but get some porridge
Don't you cry please just deny.

Finnley Thomas (11)
Higher Failsworth Primary School, Failsworth

The Attack

As I drifted off to sleep
I closed my eyes to dream a dream.
As I soared through the sky,
I could see a war happening with fairies and wizards.
Bang! An explosion came from the ground
Where magical beings can be found.
The war ended and the wizards won
No more fairies in the land.

Harrison Rouse (10)

Higher Failsworth Primary School, Failsworth

The Best Dream

Last night, I had a dream
But not one with fairies and dragons
One with my favourite team (United)
Playing football, the best I can,
Scoring goals like a goal machine
Living my best life in Old Trafford's paradise
With my favourite players, playing all night
Meeting all the legends.

Sofia Mills (10)
Higher Failsworth Primary School, Failsworth

Just A Nap

There was a flood in the woods, there were clowns,
That had drowned and there was no one there so I was scared,
Because I dared to scare a clown that was there with red,
Hair who had a bear that threw a pear, I blinked,
Fast then I felt a draught,
Then I realised it was just a nap.

Ethan Olive (10)
Higher Failsworth Primary School, Failsworth

Dragons

Every night in my dreams I see dragons fly by
Tails of the starlight and the sun shining bright
The dragons live in a castle where they have a king
named Mastle
Every night I leave half hoping they will stay
Perhaps next year they'll come from the planet beyond
to make a bond...

Muhammad Danial (11)
Higher Failsworth Primary School, Failsworth

Astronaut

As I drift off to sleep I hear my mum shout, "Brush your teeth!"
Soon enough I'm in a land of dreams going into the galaxy,
Ten thousand stars I can see I am left alone up here it's just me,
But suddenly I hear a scream realising it was just a dream.

Ben Ward (11)
Higher Failsworth Primary School, Failsworth

Manchester United

M an U vs Liverpool today,

A really big ball, a small net,

N o one can score, not today,

C an you hear us, Rashford's top,

H ear you of course, what?

E rr referee, run, the ball on fire,

S omeone help just then the sun,

T ouched the stadium, *bang* the ball popped,

E r mama mia here we go again,

R un like the sky sun tick,

U rgh guys nothing's here,

N o, we need to get out of here,

I mmediately, hurry arrgh,

T ime isn't on the clock,

E veryone come here, zoom,

D n, dn, dn a box, it opened a portal, our world let's go.

Joshua Shaw (9)
Hill Top CE Primary School, Low Moor

Space Football

S omehow, I was in space

"P erfect!" someone shouted

A nd the voices got louder with every step

C ould it be Klopp shouting?

E very second I walked, I heard Klopp.

F rom then on, I wanted the players

O ther teams were good

O thers were not as good as Liverpool

T hen, later, they let me play

"B e the striker," said Klopp. "Okay"

A ll the players loved my skills

L ater on, I hurt my leg

L eg! Oh! Then I realised I was in bed.

Bobby Hegarty (9)

Hill Top CE Primary School, Low Moor

The Big Pompeii Disaster

E arth is shaking, walls are breaking

A s I hear screaming people crying

R ight when the chaos was happening, volcano

T ime was here, house into ash and rubble

H ow did it turn barren so quick? Tremors

Q uickly started, I couldn't

U nderstand what was happening, the Sims all had

A horrible way of dying, birds looming in the

K ingdom of Pompeii, all I could see was smoke,

E veryone was gone.

S oon I woke up and found myself in bed.

Rayane (9)
Hill Top CE Primary School, Low Moor

Space Football

S uch an amazing goal
P ace onto the ball
A nd it was a really good shot
C ould it be their best player
E nd of the match there was a fight.

F antastic win
O ne day I dreamt of being a footballer
O n his debut, he scored
T he man of the match
B all was rolling to him
A good goal for him
L ong pass to him
L ovely goal.

Frankie Batterfield (9)

Hill Top CE Primary School, Low Moor

Taylor Swift

T aylor Swift is my favourite singer
A s she dances and sings
Y eah, hip hip hooray, the crowd screams
L ow down screams and shouts
O r they let it out
R ound and round, songs go up and down

S wifties all around
W ay up high, way down low
I am in bed
F ast asleep, realising it was all a dream
T eddy I say goodnight as I cuddle him tight.

Faith Lupton (8)
Hill Top CE Primary School, Low Moor

Shifter

S caring people through the night, giving them a fright

H earing people from my room screaming in the night

I t turned into a monster that flew like an eagle through the air

F lying like a plane, I wanted to too, it wasn't fair!

T he monster that scares me is always out of sight

E verywhere it was flying it was night

R esting in my bed I realised it was a nightmare.

Amar Dhillon (9)
Hill Top CE Primary School, Low Moor

Fish Are Mean

F ish fight in the water
I n the water, fish are bullies
S ecretly mean fish
H orrible when they fight, the water goes swish

A way they go
R ude fights everywhere
E veryone being mean

M ucky mud everywhere
E veryone screaming
A re we going to survive?
N ight-time is creepy.

Bentley Pedder (8)
Hill Top CE Primary School, Low Moor

Space Football

S o easy to pass
P assing is good
A mazing pass
C an you score again
E nd for the first half

F antastic goal
O n the crossbar
O n the post
T he keeper is in the way
B ut it came back out and shot
A nd they scored a goal
L ovely shot
L ovely passing.

Dexter
Hill Top CE Primary School, Low Moor

I Saw Messi

I opened the door to a football pitch.

S unny day to play football
A huge pitch!
W e kicked off.

M essi was playing alongside me
E veryone cheering like birds
S uch a long shot, and tackles being made
S creaming, shouting. We won!
I saw Messi score three goals. A goal messiah!

William Hurd (9)
Hill Top CE Primary School, Low Moor

Rainbow Dog

R ainbow in the sky
A big dog to protect
I n the rain, the dog hides
N obody knows about this dog
B ow in her hair, she is happy
O verly kind
W ings as colourful as a rainbow.

D esirable dog
O verly protective
G reatest dog ever.

Baylee-Rae Womersley (9)
Hill Top CE Primary School, Low Moor

Score!

R unning down the wing, determined to score a try

U nique passes as I fly through them and score a try

G oing as fast as I can!

B ypassing the other players as I run in the air

Y elling for the ball and scored a try as the air winked.

Blake Paucher (9)
Hill Top CE Primary School, Low Moor

Untitled

F ootball is the best in the world

O pponents or the side

O n the pitch they run

T he score table

B last the ball into the goal

A ll work as a team

L aunch the ball

L eap for victory.

Memphis

Hill Top CE Primary School, Low Moor

Magic

M y little pony
A s adventurous as can be
G o walk by your favourite oak tree
I 'd love to come with you but I have homework to do
C an you come back to help me cheer up if I get sad and ghosts start to lurk?

Norah Maloney (9)
Hill Top CE Primary School, Low Moor

Dream Gaming Room

I wake up and get out of my bed, but suddenly the walls of my room are gone, and it all goes dark. Then I get the brightest light in my eye and then I see my dream game room with all my favourite games. But my mum shouts to me, it is all a dream.

Jacob Whitrick (9)
Hill Top CE Primary School, Low Moor

Swiftie

S o I love her so much
W e go to a concert
I wish she was my sister
F ire is shooting from the stage
T he crowd is shouting
I love her song
E veryone likes her.

Connie Preston (8)

Hill Top CE Primary School, Low Moor

School

S not the rotten eggs
C ool blue, shouted freeze!
H ow long can my teacher sneeze?
O h, go look in the cupboard
O h no, there is Covid-19
L onely in school, very sad.

Alyssa Rose Godfrey (9)
Hill Top CE Primary School, Low Moor

Fairy

F luttering fairies sparkle within

A s they dance and sing

I sit on my chair, just to lie

R ight underneath the golden sky

Y ou and me sing a song so just come along.

Skye Oakley (9)
Hill Top CE Primary School, Low Moor

The Life Of Dreams

Life of dreams,
Stay here with me,
I'll protect you with all my heart,
Don't disappear, my future is before me.

I barely get to see you,
A dream that seems so short,
But a dream so sweet.

The memory and feelings,
That always feels sublime,
Frozen for all time,
I just think back and smile.

My dream, you have invaded my soul,
Like a thief in the night,
You stole my heart,
You stroll around my mind, your face like art.

For all I have bid goodbye,
Slowly fading in the rising sun,
Hold fast to dreams,
For dreams will die.

Life of dreams,
Stay here with me,
I'll protect you with all my heart,
Don't disappear, my future is before me.

Jarrin Hussain (10)
Midfield Primary School, St Paul's Cray

Just A Dream

Every single day I dream of doing gymnastics,
And in every dream I follow tactics.
To my surprise I win, until I realise it's a dream,
Even with all the balancing on the beam.

Then I wake up with a happy feeling,
And I am ready for the day, shouting and squealing.
Until I realise I am not flexible,
And even a split is unbearable.

I dream of swinging on the bars and sticking it,
And all the jumping from the vault and also sticking it.
Even all the rhythm,
And everything is just a dream.

Don't get carried away by a dream,
Even if it includes you balancing on a beam.
Even all vaults, the bars and beams,
Remember, a dream is just a dream.

Esther Ayomikun Iranloye (10)
Midfield Primary School, St Paul's Cray

Features Of The Future

I wish I could see,
What will happen to me,
I want to act, dance, sing,
What will the future bring?

I want to take a chance,
To be on stage, to sing, to dance!
This is the choice I want to make,
And the chance I need to take.

I dream about this at night,
I'm glad I don't get stage fright!
On stage, I like being me,
I like being happy, I like being free.

All I wanted was to perform,
I never wanted anything more,
This is my hope, this is my plan,
My own future is in my own hands.

Charlotte Muller (9)
Midfield Primary School, St Paul's Cray

Midnight Horse

My weary head hits the pillow,
Dreams of the magnificent Midnight start to flow.

The flowing mane, the wispy tail,
Midnight's elegance will never fail.

Sparkling eyes like magic stars in the sky,
I wish these dreams would never die.

When midnight comes and it starts to rain,
You are the only one who's in my brain.

I feel free upon Midnight's graceful back,
Roaming wildly on our beautiful track.

A magic world under the magic beam,
But is everything as magic as it seems?

Emily Spittles (10)
Midfield Primary School, St Paul's Cray

In My Dreams

In my dreams
I see my family singing and
dancing with cheer
My dog running and panting
Barking to hear
One by one we all run
We are all having fun
Magic dust from above, is it for me? Is it for us?
Scatter, scatter magic dust
Rainbow unicorns jumping, sparkling bright with light
Laughter and cheer
I want to see them every night
But suddenly, they disappear
Maybe I will see them next year.

Sophie Anderson (9)
Midfield Primary School, St Paul's Cray

The Moon Shines

Sometimes I wake up within a
Dream and it makes me
Barely breathe.
Then I see the shiny
Sky glistening to
Set me free
Stars twirling and the moon
Shining
Then I get to see
The moon and then
I see a shiny spoon
Meanwhile, I see a raccoon
Then I hear a big boom
In my own room
The moon is glistening
So much and my mum hears me
So she starts listening and
I go to bed.

Hollie Anna Rynne (10)
Midfield Primary School, St Paul's Cray

Astronaut

A man who was an astronaut

S ometimes he would like to go

T o a planet full of kindness

R eal love and friendship grow

O bviously, I wouldn't go to Venus

N or will I go to Jupiter or Mars

A way from Earth

U p in the sun like stars

T o my lovely destiny.

Tony Friend (10)

Midfield Primary School, St Paul's Cray

Dreams

D reams. What dream shall I choose?
R ight there! I'll be on a cruise!
E xtra food, an added bonus!
A rctic shores up to the Caribbean!
M assive waves roar as we sail the Atlantic!
S uddenly, I find out I'm at home in bed!

Zak Souami (10)
Midfield Primary School, St Paul's Cray

Wizards In A Dream

W aving up my wand so high,

I love the sparkling sky,

Z oom over the night skies,

A bove the delicious pies,

R ide over the big wand,

D ream the awesome pond,

S ave every memory.

Anishwar Chellappan (10)

Midfield Primary School, St Paul's Cray

Tasty Night

Tasty nights,
I sleep tight,
I close my eyes,
I wave goodnight to the skies,
Dreaming of treats tonight,
Hoping no bed bugs bite.

Florence Wright (10)
Midfield Primary School, St Paul's Cray

Tropical Paradise

T errific cocktails I see on the beach; yum, yum, yum, that's for me!

R ocky mountains I see in the distance, wowee!

O ctopuses squirting ink in the sea,

P owerful waves splish-splashing me,

I see crabs crawling around,

C razy waves crashing against the rocks,

A mazing views, is that all I can see?

L ovely food that is scrumptious; that's for me,

P irates emerge from the sea,

A crobats dance in the sea,

R ainbows in the sky,

A nd I see lovely flowers for me,

D inner out tonight yes, yes, yes!

I love cocktails,

S uper sunny on the beach,

E legant massages!

Liberty Taylor (9)
Mobberley CE Primary School, Mobberley

The Dark Forest

Me and my friends Daisy and Savannah,
We went to the forest at night!
We were creeped out!
It was creepy, dark and so, so tight!
And then we were lost, lost!
We had walked so far and now sleeping,
Daisy was already sleeping, but me and Savannah hadn't,
We couldn't.
But Savannah had, how could she have fallen asleep?
It was a wolf!

Finally it was the morning,
When did I fall asleep?
The wolf had gone but when?

Wait, where is Daisy?
Did the wolf eat her?
Oh no.

We walked further,
Me and Savannah were trying to find Daisy,
No sign of her, we started to get worried.

We finally found her, she was finding food.

Thank gosh she was alive!
"Let's go home," I said.
Savannah and Daisy said, "Yes."
From now on we are never going to that forest ever again.
"Yes," said Daisy and Savannah.

Emily McIntyre (8)
Mobberley CE Primary School, Mobberley

Ten Nightmares

1. Now I stand alone in the dead of night
2. I look around this dark hell and get a fright
3. Giant monsters surround me, which I dread
4. Help me, I beg you! These children are dead
5. *Thud!* Something's here. I hear a loud sound
6. My worst fear – a grinning killer clown
7. Aliens are invading. They take my family
8. Running for my life. I might climb that tree
9. Everyone is hypnotised. Then I hear a howl
10. Should the story end here? Yes... I'm dead now.

Emily Sellars-Rooney (10)
Mobberley CE Primary School, Mobberley

My Perfect Score

Me and my teammates cheer and cheer,
As we enter nearer and nearer to the Olympic year,
When we get in, it's my turn on the beam,
Nervous and scared, I do my mount-on and before I know it,
I stick my flick and get my perfect score!
Outstanding, I make my way to the bars,
I go and jump up to the big bar.
Finally, I remember to tuck in my back tuck off bars,
After I get my perfect score.
Next the most challenging of all - vault!
I run fast enough not to make a single mistake.
Amazingly I get another perfect score.
My perfect score (30) is just me!

Louisa Todor (8)
Mobberley CE Primary School, Mobberley

The Imaginary

I see a tree with windows, but wait, there are doors.
Oh, how terrible. I'm by myself!
I do not know where I am.
Maybe in the faraway tree.
But strangely, I'm two emotions,
I'm frightened and excited at the same time!
It is a fairy!
Her name is Mystic.
But then the fairy says,
"Hug the tree and put your ear next to it."
I do and the trees are talking to me.
My biggest fear is clowns,
I want to wake up now!
I'm alive! I'm awake!
That's better.

Hope Jones (8)
Mobberley CE Primary School, Mobberley

The Sky

As I close my eyes,
I begin to rise,
I look down on the city below,
I wave goodbye but say hello,
To the mystic land, what could it be?
I look around as my ideas begin to flee,
When the sun comes up, flowers grow,
As the sun goes down, the wind starts to blow,
I see the full moon rising and hear a frightening howl,
The only thing I can think is I am definitely dead now,
But then I wake up, safe in my bed,
Will I go there again in the future?

Hettie Taylor (10)
Mobberley CE Primary School, Mobberley

My First Day Of Pirate School

When I moved house, I had to move school. I was shaking with nerves. Wednesday was the day I would start. My mum told me to get a good night's rest because tomorrow was my big day.

It was 7am. I was getting ready for school and it was at the beach. Our school was on a ship. We were on the ship and the teacher was very strict.

Three hours in, she was making me walk the plank. Once I fell into the sea, a fairy saved me and I got taken to Fairy Land with my mum and dad forever.

Frankie Cummings (8)
Mobberley CE Primary School, Mobberley

My Nightmares

In my nightmares, I'm alone,
Somewhere near, a body gets thrown,
Bodies lie on the floor, unmoving,
Monsters bang on the cages, waiting for them to be removed,
As they're freed, a monster gives a loud scream,
They tie me above a pot that starts to bubble and steam,
But, with a *whoosh*, my nightmare world falls away,
And all the nasty monsters have to pay,
Then we all shout, "Hooray!"

Zach Saunders (11)
Mobberley CE Primary School, Mobberley

High In The Sky

High in the sky, I can see the white clouds,
High in the sky, I can see the birds crowd,
High in the sky, I go up, up, up like a piano tone,
High up here is my comfort zone,
High in the azure sky, I can see the world shine,
High in the sky, there is no moon or wine,
High in the sky, there is no boundary to see,
High in the clouds is where I want to be.

Ed Hargreaves (11)
Mobberley CE Primary School, Mobberley

Graveyard Dogs

Lost in a place far away from home.
I see graves with muddy paw prints all over, bloody skulls.
I'm shaking.
I hear creepy music getting louder, louder and louder!
My spine starts to shiver, I fall to the ground and
Ah! I wake up in pink, fluffy blankets with dogs on me.
This feels weird.
I think I... I think I... I think I might
Die!

Matilda Hargreaves (9)
Mobberley CE Primary School, Mobberley

Tucked Into Bed

D ancing swiftly on a cloud,
R avenous snakes hiss oh so loud,
E ventually realise I'm just dreaming,
A mazingly I can fly in the sky,
M agically here I'm the boss, I'm the king,
I can swim as fast as a dolphin,
N o idea why I'm here,
G ot in a car, but I can't steer!

Nat Kirkwood (11)
Mobberley CE Primary School, Mobberley

Olympics

I can see judges surrounding me with pressure as you
can see,
I am with my teammates like there's nowhere else to
be,
Right now, I'm on the beam, too scared to scream!
I feel overwhelmed!
But I get my perfect score,
I am so happy, surprised and amazed!
See you on my next journey for more!

Charlotte Northover (7)
Mobberley CE Primary School, Mobberley

Super City

In my dreams every night,
As Manchester City started the fight,
Man United ran with fright.

Man City get a foul,
But then it ends up in a row,
And Haaland heads the ball.

As I wake in the morning,
I get really excited to watch the game,
For it is my favourite thing.

Dylan Waterfield (11)
Mobberley CE Primary School, Mobberley

A Miracle

I look around and see,
This is not where I am meant to be.
But this is cool, because what I can see is amazing,
Just wait and see.

It is a forest with towering trees,
Fluffy clouds that blow in the breeze.
Onwards I venture, and then it meets my eye.

A miracle!

Ellen Jones (11)
Mobberley CE Primary School, Mobberley

My Dream Came True

My name is Lola,
I like fairies.
My friend's name is Mary,
We had a sleepover.
She had elves and they came to life.
Two of them were called Thandi and Candy,
And I have two fairies, Emily and Melony.
They came to life,
It came true,
The dream that I have been dreaming.

Daisy Middleditch (8)
Mobberley CE Primary School, Mobberley

Untitled

F orever I've been waiting

O sman appears

O ver there, I see something

T he terrible teams appear

B *oom!* Fernandes scores

A rchie Gray appears. What a defender!

L iving at Trafford

L iving the life!

Archie Murrell (8)
Mobberley CE Primary School, Mobberley

Football Freedom

In my dreams every night,
Footballers run down the left and right.
I see them dancing, galloping away,
But then they're gone, not here to stay.
As number four makes a clear,
Everybody starts to cheer.
Now it is morning,
I wake up yawning.

Henry Taylor (11)
Mobberley CE Primary School, Mobberley

Clowns

C reepy clowns are the worst,

L oud clowns I do not like,

O vernight they like to scare,

W riggling clowns like to squirm,

N ightmarish clowns like to fright,

S cary clowns are in my nightmares...

Amelia-Rose Stapleton (11)

Mobberley CE Primary School, Mobberley

Dreamland

In a mystical dreamland, in the air,
There is a fairy sprinkling fairy dust over there,
I need to jump from cloud to cloud without falling down,
With a fluffy, small dog, which is brown,
I feel curious about this land.

Olivia Marshall (8)
Mobberley CE Primary School, Mobberley

Dreamy Beach

B eing on a beach,

E legant waves and cold sea,

A mazing views all around me,

C razy waves crashing on me,

H ot, hot sand on my feet, always in my dream every night.

Poppy Nicholson (8)

Mobberley CE Primary School, Mobberley

My Best Score

I'm trying to get a ten out of ten,
But I can never get my score if I don't work hard.
I will try, but I never get it.
Sometimes I get sad, but I keep working hard.

Liviana Baines (8)
Mobberley CE Primary School, Mobberley

Five Lines Of My Dream

D reaming in a garden

R unning with my friend

E very day we play

A m I dreaming?

M y mum just said I am, I don't want to leave.

Poppy Norbury (10)

Mobberley CE Primary School, Mobberley

My Football Dream

In my dream,
I was playing football with my friends
And with my favourite football players,
And I felt amazing on my favourite field
But I wished it was real.

Ronny Owens (8)
Mobberley CE Primary School, Mobberley

Five Dreams

D reaming in the sky
R emembering I'm in bed
E verything is nice
A m I awake now?
M y feet are on fluffy clouds.

Juliette Hurley (10)
Mobberley CE Primary School, Mobberley

Unidragons

Once, I saw something flying in the air. It had quite a long horn and quite long hair so I shouted out to the creature, "Hey, over here!" But the creature was gone but then it reappeared. So I shouted again, "Can you hear me?"

"Yes," it said dearly.

I walked on to see but instead it followed me. "What are you?" I called out politely.

"I'm a unidragon," the creature called but rudely.

I walked away in disappointment not knowing what a unidragon was but I thought of something. The reason I could not see was because he put a spell on me! I ran home and grabbed my goggles and put them on. My mother stopped me and sang me a song. After that, I went back to the spot I saw the unidragon. "Hello!" I shouted out to the distance of mist. The unidragon appeared again. "What's your name?" I called out. "Who cares? But did you notice my mane?" he replied. That's when I noticed that this unidragon was just a big show-off. So I walked away back home and told my parents about it and the spell it put on me. That night, I dreamed of my day but couldn't quite remember it so maybe I was dreaming...

Coral-Olivia Brown (9)
North Town Primary School, Taunton

The Lost Superpower

On the dried riverbank where the sun is bright,
Lives a girl in a cottage so happy and kind,
The flowers blooming are a lovely sight,
She sits watching the dazzling sunlight,

A stroke goes through her full of power,
And she feels a powerful bright silent light,
She feels like she's on a high tower,
Waiting to find a way out.

The hustle shakes violently,
And her veins begin to shake,
All of a sudden silence reigns,
For her power breaks through her veins,

She tries to fight it but it comes back through,
A vicious ice speck collides within,
And her exit is a pile of goo,
Letting her be free to be.

Jasmine Mcevansoneya (8)
North Town Primary School, Taunton

Easy Win

It's an easy win when you can fly
If the goalie gets scared you fly to the rescue.
When you play up front just kick the ball in the air,
No one will get it off you, it will be an easy win.

Every club comes in for big offers,
Even small clubs can pay a lot but for the season
I'm still at the same club for now (Liverpool)
Score the winning goal in the World Cup for my country
(England).

Finally, I've retired at the age of 45.
I've become a famous writer
And I'm still writing about me and my easy wins.
It's an easy win writing similar stories,
Also the same, it's a very easy win.

Jack Rose (8)
North Town Primary School, Taunton

I Dream, I Dream

I dream, I dream
To save the Earth,
From the swelling troubles that are about to give birth,
I'll crush them down like a meteorite,
Then say goodbye on a space-bound flight.

I dream, I dream
That when I grow up,
I'll show the world that it's not quite full up,
'Cause little children like me, our voices aren't hums,
People need to know we're not dirt from their thumbs.

I dream, I dream
That paint was alive,
Coming home from school
And when you arrive,
You see a painted penguin, jumping up and down,
Looking like a dancing clown.

Carys Perry (9)
North Town Primary School, Taunton

Crazy Dream!

Welcome to my crazy dream
Floating on a custard cream
In a sea of melted cheese
My only friends are giant fleas.

We are sailing to a land
Made of actual golden sand.

Eventually, we get to shore
And on the beach, there is a store
Selling worm and snail pies
Run by a dragon with three eyes.

He turns around and says to me
"Here, please take this magic key"
Then we ride upon a snake
And dive into a chocolate lake
There we find a silver chest
I use the key and...

Suddenly I wake up snoring; hopefully today's more
boring!

Rufus Ennals (8)
North Town Primary School, Taunton

Queen

I once had a dream,
When I was queen.

It was really cool,
To have a waterslide and pool.

I loved having twenty Border collies,
I was free! No more eating veg! (Even my favourite,
broccoli.)

Everywhere I went, I'd get a ride home,
Ahh, what a life, feeling majestic on the throne.

Wherever I went, I'd get a lift;
I was best friends with Taylor Swift.

Every day, I'd eat golden steak,
Being queen was really great.

Until the time came when I heard my mom say,
"Alexa, wake up! You've got school today."

Alexandra Slonska De Ostoja (10)
North Town Primary School, Taunton

Tonto The Crazy Cat!

Oh my, what a night,
Crazy Tonto is here to delight,
He's fast as a flash around the room,
But with a blink, he vanishes across the gloom.
He rushes upstairs around his mum,
But when I appear he quickly goes outside with a move.
But when I grab a pack of sweets,
Crazy Tonto whizzes to the beat.
"Oh dear," I go, "you Crazy Tonto,
Now you're it for the game of tag.
But I need to give you sweet treats,
So you can't be Crazy Tonto again!"

Areeya Ketnil (8)
North Town Primary School, Taunton

The Wishing Well

One dim forest,
On a dark blue night,
When the moon is cold,
When the stars are bright.

Once I wished upon a magical well,
Don't ask about my wish; I'll never tell,
When I chucked my wish it tore me apart,
Now it is in the well, not in my heart.

Sometimes I wonder about my wish,
Whether it is swimming like a fish,
Or it was swollen by venomous adders,
But I know deep down it'll come true,
And that is all that matters.

Sonia Nikisina (8)
North Town Primary School, Taunton

Minecraft

M onsters and zombies have found us. Will we win?

I n the dungeons, late at night, scared out of our skin

N etherite swords and axes flying through the air

E veryone anxiously running everywhere

C an Hugo and I make it through the night?

R ushing and running into the great fight

A life is gone and nine more to go

F erociously, we battle. Heroes, let's go

T rying not to perish...

Harrison Dorrill (8)
North Town Primary School, Taunton

Dragon Dream

Every night, I have visions, bright,
Of dragons flying in the sky,
They get higher and higher,
Breathing flames of fire,
Their wings flapping,
Their claws tapping.

The moon smiled and the stars danced,
Whilst all around me dragons pranced,
As they circled a nearby tree they looked so free.

Suddenly, I saw an amber flash,
In the distance the animals dash,
I wake up panicking in the darkness.

Luna Raby (8)
North Town Primary School, Taunton

Magical Land

M aking things
A noise deep in the woods
G oing to check out the noise
I entered a magic land
"C an I do something here?" I asked a fairy
"A im for the flowers, when it comes," she said
L akes are white

L and is green
A nd skies are bright, I want to live here
N eedingly
"D ay here is awesome."

Alina Meshack (8)
North Town Primary School, Taunton

Once Upon A Dream

In a dream,
I was sliding down a rainbow.
I landed in a magical garden,
Where a flower garden waved at me.

I was walking on a whitened beach,
The sand was white as snow.
The sea was clear as a mirror,
Which made my heart full of joy.

Then a horse was flying.
I went on it.
When I went higher,
I saw the horse was changing colours.

If I am lucky, I hope it comes again.

Jewel Jithu (9)
North Town Primary School, Taunton

The Boxer Shark

I swim alone when I fight,
There's no such thing as my bite,
Then I use my left, followed by my right,
I am Meg the boxer shark.

When I'm in the ring,
I wait for the bell to ding,
My opponent, Great Shark White,
Puts up a great fight.

When I swim down Reef Street,
I'm not afraid of who I meet,
My fins are always out of reach,
I am Meg, the boxer shark.

Joey Sawyer (9)
North Town Primary School, Taunton

My Fairy Friends

My dreams take me into the fairies,
Flying like a star in the sky,
Their dust falling like confetti at a party,
Their wings flutter quickly like a bird in flight,
And they take me on an amazing adventure.

Oh fairies, how amazing and small you are,
You take me through every little step of my dreams
and my goals,
Where I will be what I should be.

Kayla Nyika (8)
North Town Primary School, Taunton

Magic Dreams

M agic dreams, magnificent dreams,
A wake me,
G lowing stars,
I nvisible world,
C ries of the clouds.

D azzling rainbows,
R ise above the moon,
E ntering the golden gates,
A mazing shooting stars,
M elting marshmallows,
S tars are shining.

Daria Marita (7)
North Town Primary School, Taunton

A Dog

There was a dog named Blueberry.
He was a lovely dog.
I liked to hold his tail.
He was so cute that I cried.
He was my best friend.
Blueberry loved it when I scratched his neck.
He was always asking for more.
He was asking for more and more.
And I laughed 'cause of the fun.
I loved Blueberry so much.

Maja Wawrzyniak (8)
North Town Primary School, Taunton

A Cricketer

In my dreams every night
I see myself as a cricketer bowler,
With a ball bowled out to get a wicket,
I see my team members around me
And two batsmen in front of me,
Sometimes I see myself as a batsman,
Playing to help my team win.

Thank you.

Abhinav Binu (8)
North Town Primary School, Taunton

At Space

Chasing each other,
Like rockets,
Make it fun,
With smiling stars,
Playing and playing,
All day long,
Flipping, throwing,
Passing and giggling,
Floating through the clouds,
10, 9, 8, 7...
Back to Earth,
I'm in my bed!

Okitha Ranaweera (7)
North Town Primary School, Taunton

Dream Poems

My house is just a dream and your house is
Small in real life.
I have a trampoline on a dream team.
Love is love in my dream.
I dream of that day when I see you now.
A dream that I don't spend my daydreaming.

Hugo
North Town Primary School, Taunton

Dinosaur Dragons

I was one with my teddy
His name was Eddy
Till I teleported to a land
Far more than bland
With dinos and dragons
I was gazing for this world was amazing
So much, I couldn't stop gazing
Even stars couldn't stay still
For a second I thought I felt ill
I now wanted to explore
Because I saw a claw
I never wanted to leave
But couldn't believe
My parents were nearly up
So I picked up my stuff
And said goodbye to the dinos and dragons.

Molly Bungay (9)
Stanton Harcourt CE Primary School, Stanton Harcourt

Cats Lie Everywhere

Cats in bed, being fed,
Wake up yawning, with the sound of morning.
Going down and all around,
Then back to bed, within the shed,
Cats pounce and chase a mouse.
With a paw, use a claw,
To catch breakfast, one must be first,
And have a purse.
In winter they always lie
But in August they never cry.
Cats lie everywhere.

Tenuki Lokugamhewa (8)
Stanton Harcourt CE Primary School, Stanton Harcourt

Royalty

R umbling river,

O verflowing ocean,

Y apping yaks,

A dventuring apes,

L oving letters,

T angling tails,

Y ou're royalty.

Georgie Day (9)

Stanton Harcourt CE Primary School, Stanton Harcourt

Space And Life

Galaxy meandering
Morning blazing
Milky Way passing
Age gaining
Small starting
Essential warming
Black hole lurking
Shadow cascading.

Olga Jastrzebska (7)
Stanton Harcourt CE Primary School, Stanton Harcourt

Puppies Are The Best

P layful little ones,

U nlikely to not jump?

P eople sometimes have them,

P eople not like me!

Y ay, I love puppies!

Livi Brown (9)
Stanton Harcourt CE Primary School, Stanton Harcourt

The Champion

Dancers,
Steady, fun,
Dancing, swaying, winning,
Always fun to dance with,
Boogie time!

Elissa Hammonds (8)
Stanton Harcourt CE Primary School, Stanton Harcourt

Malamanders

M alamander is chasing me for I have, like a creep, picked up its egg.

A s I run, I find a fisherman's hut and enter. *Slam!* I shut the door, it smells like fish and feels rough.

L apping at the sides of the hut, the creepy, slimy Malamander tries to dig its way in.

A t the sight of me, the fat, black cat yowls at me.

M y first human sound that I hear is a fisherman, shouting from the top of the stairs from the old, ramshackle, tall, three-storey building.

A s I see the first pair of clunky, dirty boots, I realise that I'm in his house.

N obody meant to enter a fisherman's hut...

D evilishly, he smiles and with one big, bony hand picks up a two-sided axe, it stares at me.

E rily, he clomps down the stairs, sounding like a madman.

R aging, he slams down his axe onto me sitting in a corner, *bam!*

S uddenly, I wake up at home with my cat slowly sniffing at my face.

Isabella Frederick-Martinez (10)
The King's School, Gloucester

The Lost Puppy!

Down in the street, where no one knows,
But that's where the lost puppy goes,
He lives alone, a sad life,
Where you need to spend hours for a meal.

The lost puppy, scared as can be,
Gets bullied by a big dog who looks at me,
He chases him through the city,
Oh, what a pity!

Snarling and growling through the town,
Chasing and running down,
In the tunnels,
As he finally was as fast as ever.

Boom! Crash! You see a car and a girl,
And it goes dark,
It goes blurry,
Beep! Beep! Beep! And so on.

Suddenly, you're in the shelter!
And you see a girl,
She's staring straight at you,
But you can't move, and you can only hear,
"Yay, we're taking him home!"

Your worst nightmare has just come true,
You are going with a human,
But you say to yourself,
"Be optimistic, maybe it's a good family, one who cares."

On the first night, they seem to like you,
But they never feed you or play,
You get tired and weak,
And they call the vet.

And you're happy again,
The vet takes you away,
To the shelter,
"Why?" you wail,
You want to scream, but can't.

You start to feel hopeless,
Because you are there for weeks,
Trying to get out,
Until another girl approaches you.

She's like a warm, kind person who you want to hug,
You feel it in her,
You finally know she's saved you.

She was perfect,
She acted like an angel from Heaven,
For days, months, weeks, never bored.

That's the life of the lost puppy.

Abbi Navaratnam (10)
The King's School, Gloucester

My Mythical Creature

M y mythical creature lives in a forest that smells of strawberries,
Y ou would never, ever find him.

M ango is his name,
Y ou would always find him tame,
T aking on this mighty creature would give you a fright,
H e breathes out fire so bright you wouldn't want to fight,
I always try to be his friend,
C an he be too crazy to make it end?
A ttacking my friend would hurt him badly,
L ike putting a pin on a chair, that wouldn't be fair!

C rashing the forest disturbs the people,
R ecreating peace between the people explains he is not evil,
E lephants are smaller than him,
A nd lots of people call him Tim,
T oday he still lives in the forest,
U ntil he knocks a tree down into the town,
R eading is his favourite thing,
E xercising him is like walking to school on wheels it's so hard!

Sabrina Stratford (10)

The King's School, Gloucester

My Magnificent World And You

M y world is the best with you by my side,
Y ou will never forget!

M e and my place are the best of friends,
A s close as the world, with a big hug,
G o if you dare, you will never survive,
N ever come back or you will be dead!
I f you come again, you will be gone in a flash!
F urther that you travel, you will never find me, fill up
with anger and rage, then lie down with happiness,
I f you succeed, you are the best!
C ome with me and you will find a magical place,
E veryone knows about it, so come right in,
N ever give up or surrender,
T ry your hardest, you will always succeed.

W ill you care if you go back home?
O n the first day of your life, you come here with joy,
R oll over here and join us,
L earn more and more to strengthen your heart,
D o your best, you know you can!

A nd you will be the best you can ever be,

N ever go, we love you so,

D o go, but always remember me.

Y ou smell like lovely rose bushes,

O ff you go now!

U ntil you die, just go to your home but always remember me!

Eliza Humber (10)

The King's School, Gloucester

Jungle

Running through the jungle with its waving trees,
I see a lonely leopard, who wants to come with me,
We start to have a chat like no one has before,
We carry on running through the lovely jungle.

Walking through the jungle with the leopard by my side,
Zoom! I see a cheeky cheetah,
Who happily joins our pride, he shows us,
His running skills, which impress me,
Then we carry on walking through the amazing jungle.

Jogging through the jungle with my friends,
Grumble! We see a hungry hyena who wants to join for tea,
We love the things he said,
Then we all go to bed,
In the beautiful jungle.

We wake up in the morning,
With my friends, as well,
I am so happy, I feel like I could fly,
It feels like a dream, I cannot lie
In the damp and chirping jungle.

Then, we run with a butterfly,
We try to keep up,
We try, we try, we try, then with the sun shining bright
We leave the magical, jungle.

Harvey Dodson (10)
The King's School, Gloucester

Real Madrid, Here I Am

R unning around, as fast as a Concord
E ating teams like a T-rex eating herbivores
A ccurate shots, as accurate as a calculator
L ifting trophies, as many as the people on Earth.

M bappé is here in a flash
A nd we'll keep winning shiny, golden trophies
D estroying teams in a click of a finger
R eaching history for our amazing signings
I gniting our team's hopeful spirits
D reaming, dreaming that one day I will be part of
them too.

H opes are as high as Mount Everest
E ngland born, England roots
R eaching the sparkly lit up Bernabéu
E xcited as I never would be again.

I had done it, the stadium was reaching out to me, it
hugged me and said, "You're home!"

A ctually the first time I ever played for a big club
M oving from England was the only option.

Oliver Odufuwa (9)
The King's School, Gloucester

136

In A Magical World

In the night, I fall into a magical world,
Which is a bright and colourful world,
In front of me, I can see unicorns, mermaids and fairies,
Bright, colourful mermaid tails swim past me.

Unicorns with bright, beautiful, rainbow horns,
Fly past me with delight,
And if you walk through the city,
You will come across a gigantic, beautiful rainbow.

With a huge, gigantic, cheesy smile on its face,
As big as the happiest person in the world,
All of a sudden, some people come on flying carpets,
Zooming! Whizzing past me!

Suddenly, Freya, Ella, Izzy and Evie appear,
But in their pyjamas!
Then, a mermaid asks us to climb on the rainbow,
It is hard work as it is as tall as a skyscraper.

When I woke up,
I was sad but relieved,
Because it all was a dream,
It's an experience never to forget!

Molly Smart (10)
The King's School, Gloucester

Earth And Fire

As we line up in rows with huge armadillos,
The Fire Nation comes,
They throw huge balls of fire.
The boulders that are thrown to block the fire squeal in pain,
But the Fire Nation never stops.

We try to stop them, but they are too powerful.
They knock down our tower with all the children in.
Suddenly, I get knocked out cold.

As I wake up to the smell of smoke
To the groan of my friends and family
Lying on the floor
Hurt from battle,
I get ready to fight again.

My armour is so heavy,
I see everything on fire.
My head fills with anger,
I see people fighting on the cliff.
I sprint towards it,
I start beaming the Fire Nation soldiers with small pebbles.

I get too close to the edge,
And they kick me hard in the stomach.
I tumble down into the sea.
I cannot breathe,
I cannot move,
Everything goes black,
Black forever.

Fred Beavon-Keenan (10)
The King's School, Gloucester

Ducks Through A Window

I go into a brand-new resturant,
I sit down with my mum,
I then order my dinner,
I wait for it to come,
I see three ducks through a window,
They quack and call to me,
I ask my mum politely if I can answer them,
She says no.

They call over and over again,
I plead and beg my mum,
I'm very sad when she says no.

My mum goes to the toilet,
She says, "You must wait here."
I sneak away to find the ducks,
It turns out they're not there!

I look around and find them,
They are in a duck alleyway,
They want to give me something,
I ask, "What?"

They give me a beautiful, wooden duckling model as cute as a kitten,
I say thanks and walk away,
I go back to show my mum,
She says, "That's enough disappearing for today."

Sebastian Le Page (9)
The King's School, Gloucester

Nightmare

In the night in the wood,
Clowns and demons that give you a fright,
Dark and gloomy you hear something,
The sky is a ship of pirates sailing this night,
You want to get away but clowns are chasing you all night.

You've lost your friend in the gloomy forest,
Your dog's by your side,
You see a car and run for your life,
You jump in and leave your dog behind,
Rumble, rumble, the engine starts,
You speed off in the dark.

Your exhaust going *pop! Bang! Vroom* and *zoom*,
You went the wrong way, you're in mid-air,
You just jumped off a cliff, is this the end?

You wake on the floor, you think you're out.
You open the tent and...
You're stuck for life and you're doomed for life.
It's game over.

Theodore Currie (10)
The King's School, Gloucester

Changed

I stood in a magical world,
The breeze running through my hair,
A smooth, pretty path was protected by the warmth of
my shoes,
There were bright, blooming flowers everywhere!

My friend was as squiddly as a Year Seven girl,
Happy, healthy people roamed the streets,
The trees waved,
The sun winked,
But the air (mood) changed in a millisecond.

I turned to see my friend disintegrate!
And I heard a faint scream,
The healthy, happy people turned gloomy,
All the pretty flowers died like the people's spirits,
The houses were abandoned, wood blocked the
windows.

I saw spooky, scary zombies coming from the border,
I heard the groans coming towards me,
And something grabbed me...
Ding, ding, I'm late for school!

Kitty Dare (9)
The King's School, Gloucester

Meadow Ghost Cats!

I woke up in a land,
A land of big, fluffy ghost cats.
I turned around as fast as a cheetah and saw a
glowing light.
A butterfly flew upon my nose and lit up my face with
joy.

In this land I sat,
Stroking a snow-white cat.
In this land I sat,
As happy as can be.

The butterfly right by my side,
The sun screaming painfully at my eyes.
A sight stole my eye.

A purple fizzing potion,
Soaring into view,
That fizzy, purple potion
Into my mouth it flew!

I had a bubbly feeling,
Rushing through my veins.
And *boom!* the next sensation,
Smacked me in the face.

I turned around to find myself in the middle of outer space.
I bounced around happily, joyfully! It all felt so real,
Until I woke up.

Evangeline Walker (9)
The King's School, Gloucester

Predator

In a jungle miles away,
There's a creature hidden in the day.
Its face is hidden behind a mask,
Hidden from dismay.

With a slim, ugly figure,
An ancient form.
A build quite like a human's,
But a face long ago torn.

Go a few miles to the coast,
No! Take cover! Phew that was close!
That missile nearly blew up my head!
But instead went *boom!* on the sea bed.

As I take to the skies in my plane,
It looks like it has started to rain.
Maybe water, maybe hail,
Oh no! My engine has now failed!

As I descend into the trees to land,
Vine-like things snag my jet, fingers on a hand,
On a branch near me something grins,
Now I realise, it's just me and that *thing...*

James Hargreaves (9)
The King's School, Gloucester

146

The Cats And Dogs War

When I walked down a strange town street,
I did not know before,
My cats were next to me,
Walking along the dusty floor,
Then I realised the other cats,
Were also sitting there,
On the floor, or on a chair,
I saw a lot of crazy things.

Suddenly, it changed from happy to sad,
There was a war of dogs and cats,
We had to go to an air raid shelter,
We could hear big booms and big bangs and saw
nothing.

We saw a gap in the wall, as thin as a worm,
And through that, we saw planes, which had dogs in
them,
Then, a Kraken came out of the salty sea, going
forward,
And crashed onto a plane, into the grassy ground.

Then, I felt super scared in the air raid shelter,
And woke up super safe in my cosy bed.

Tom Holliday (10)
The King's School, Gloucester

Deathland

The skies are high
But at night it changes the sky's design
When you're blue, it won't be so cool
So don't think that's too good
Bang, crash, zoom, pop, there goes the clicking clock
And now it's the Earth's design way too high the time
has come
But I'm not ready, moving things from the sky
This is the time when most people die
You smell dirty and gruff
Don't ever come again
I'm only nine, it's not the time
Clowns and dolls drop from the sky
These are dreams in the land
I'm never coming to that stinky, smelly, obnoxious and
disgusting house
But I wish I was still with my best friends
Kobe, Lebron and Kevin
But suddenly I found out that I was safe at home.

Josiah Manboard (9)
The King's School, Gloucester

Dreaming Resort

D irt and seed line my house, plus some stinky dog poo,

R oaring inside the bottom of the hill, crocodiles there too,

E xplaining to me how to get in,

A nswered a crocodile, missing one shiny emerald fin,

M any people saw the castle tower,

I nching forward every hour,

"N ever mind" shouted the fat hippo ladies,

G laring at me, just like Hades.

R apidly, firing at the castle,

E ntered the queen, rushing in a hassle,

S melling, sniffing the fresh vomit air,

O oof! She got some right in her hair,

R acing for her giant, giraffe guard's arm,

T he castle is now broken sand, living in horrible harm.

Liesl Bier (10)
The King's School, Gloucester

In My Nightmares

Is it just me,
But once a week,
You turn on the light,
A sudden spark gives you a fright,
You have a nightmare!

A monster under your bed,
Ready to give you a scare,
Your carpet walks up to you,
Ready to eat your head!

It's horrible, haunting,
They're scary, savage,
They don't stop 'til they hear your scream,
They're like a giant,
As scary as the sea.

The dolls are nice and fun,
Until they rip your head off, just for fun!

Everything in your room gives you a grin,
Firstly you think it's just a dream,
You realise they're harmless really until,
You wake up with your light on,
And a terrible scream!

Rosie Worthington (10)
The King's School, Gloucester

Basketball

B oom! As I dunk on someone as tall as a tree,

A fire inside me starts as they taunt me with glee,

S uperman! They shout as I soar through the sky,

K neeling down, the other team stares at me, eye to eye,

E veryone cheers as I score my 102nd point,

T hey couldn't believe how young, new and amazing I was (they thought I had no joints),

B ut little did I know, that they would sabotage me,

A ll of a sudden, I was as small as a petty pea,

L oads of the fans started booing as loud as an ear-splitting, annoying trumpet,

L ittle did they know, I just wanted a truly scrumptious crumpet (I could smell it already!).

Charlie Elsby Harfield (10)
The King's School, Gloucester

Me And Joey In Meow Meow Land

Me and Joey in Meow Meow Land,
A world of crazy curiosity!
Me and Joey in Meow Meow Land,
As fluffy as cotton candy!

Me and Joey in Meow Meow Land,
I'm going mad!
Me and Joey in Meow Meow Land,
Joey is quietly talking to me.

Me and Joey in Meow Meow Land,
Meow! Meow! Meow! Meow!
Me and Joey in Meow Meow Land,
We wish we could stay.

Look at my hands!
They've become fluffy little paws!
Joey and I love it here,
Castles look like cats!
I smell caramel ice cream!
Joey smells delicious Doritos.

Me and Joey in Meow Meow Land,
We love it here!

Caspar Smith (9)

The King's School, Gloucester

Spiders

Each night, as I go to bed,
I dream of scary spiders, crawling across my face,
They go into my mouth with their hairy legs,
They crawl across my body, onto my legs,
They go around my body,
It feels like they're wrapping me in a massive web,
It feels like sticky glue.

Spiders can do anything to wake me up,
Then in my dream, they take me to their web nest,
There are large spiders,
But in the middle of the nest,
There is a gigantic spider,
Then, they put me under the spider,
Then, I can see its massive teeth and its red eyes,
Then, I wake up with a scream,
Argh!

Luca Grosch (9)
The King's School, Gloucester

My Cat And I On Bonfire Night

My cat and I, on Bonfire Night,
Watched as the seagulls took flight
On the big, sandy beach.
And I took a treat
Out of my bag
For my cat and I, on Bonfire Night.

I gave it to my cat,
My gorgeous, gorgeous cat.
Her soft blanket of fur,
Dazzling in the light,
And her soft, calming purr,
Helps me fall asleep, on Bonfire Night.

As we walked along the beach
We heard it! We saw it!
What a magnificent feat!
Beautiful fireworks outshining the stars
Blooming like blossoms now springing out.
That's what we did,
My cat and I, on Bonfire Night.

Amelia van Wyk (9)
The King's School, Gloucester

Nightmare

N ight, night, my mum said while tucking me in my warm, fluffy bed.

I didn't know that night, I might get a little bit of a fright.

G urgling voice I hear at the end of the pitch-black land.

H e hears me toppling over, as I try to run away.

T he monsters I see while I fling myself as far as can be.

M ore monsters fully surrounding me.

A re they gonna stay? I hope not!

R apidly, I look left, they are there, right there still.

E rily, I open my eyes to realise I'm safe at home, cosy, in my bed.

Freddie Haighway (10)
The King's School, Gloucester

The Crew

T here's a magical, wonderful crew, sailing for all the blue,

H ere in the Cloud World, the clouds dance like they're on a dance floor,

E arly in the morning, all you can see are fluffy cotton clouds,

C autiously, there's a monster pirate coming to find all the blue,

R apidly, the crew are sailing on clouds, the boat was ready,

E ven though they are getting chased, they are rolling like a Ferrari.

W herever they will be, they'll still be sailing to find all the blue.

Zac Yousif Spilsbury (10)

The King's School, Gloucester

The Bus Trip

T he bus trip, I'm going on a bus trip!
H ow will I go?
E very day of the year, I've planned.

B ut will I make it?
U h, I have an idea,
S hh, don't tell anyone, I'm going today!

T he harsh drops gobble me up, rocky roads throw me about, and the humongous, marvellous mountains stare down at me,
R eady? Let's go!
I suddenly get lost, where am I?
P oems, I can't write while driving.

Alfie Spokes (10)
The King's School, Gloucester

Dogs Everywhere

In Dog Land, there are dogs everywhere,
There are dogs running,
Dancing, flying and even playing chess.

There are dogs in the park and even at school,
There are pups everywhere.
You would never believe how cool it is,
It's as cool as a terrifying orange dragon.
You even hear "Roof, roof, roof" and "Bark, bark, bark."

A magnificent land,
You should come along and see,
The magnificent land of doggies and me.

Eddie Skivington (10)
The King's School, Gloucester

Untitled

S inging on stage, as happy as can be,
P eople laughing at me, ha ha ha,
I fall into a hole, it's dark, deep and tall,
D ark-eyed spiders crawl happily just for me,
E ventually, they are crawling up my leg,
R unning as fast as I can to leave,
S uddenly I wake up, it was all a dream.

Imogen Halliday
The King's School, Gloucester

I Fell

Skipping like quicksilver,
Falling clumsily,
Wickedly spinning toward the beckoning cliffs.

Falling off,
Calling like a lion,
Quickly losing grip.

Falling,
Screaming,
Dropping like a stone.

Landing,
Painfully,
Going to sleep forever with a crash!

Rhys Walker (10)
The King's School, Gloucester

Young Writers®
Est. 1991

YOUNG WRITERS INFORMATION

We hope you have enjoyed reading this book – and that you will continue to in the coming years.

If you're a young writer who enjoys reading and creative writing, or the parent of an enthusiastic poet or story writer, do visit our website **www.youngwriters.co.uk**. Here you will find free competitions, workshops and games, as well as recommended reads, a poetry glossary and our blog.

If you would like to order further copies of this book, or any of our other titles, then please give us a call or visit **www.youngwriters.co.uk**.

Young Writers
Remus House
Coltsfoot Drive
Peterborough
PE2 9BF
(01733) 890066
info@youngwriters.co.uk

f YoungWritersUK   **X** YoungWritersCW
⊙ youngwriterscw   **♪** youngwriterscw